EACH BRIGHT EYE

Valerie Gillies

EACH BRIGHT EYE

Selected Poems 1971–1976

CANONGATE

This selection first published in 1977
by Canongate Publishing Limited,
17 Jeffrey Street, Edinburgh.

© Valerie Gillies 1972, 1974, 1975, 1976, 1977

ISBN 0 903937 44 1   Hardback
0 903937 45 x Paperback

The publishers acknowledge the financial assistance of
the Scottish Arts Council in the publication of this volume

Printed and bound in Great Britain by
Morrison & Gibb Ltd, London and Edinburgh

Contents

Acknowledgments

I remember with gratitude the Commonwealth Scholarship which made it possible for me to live in India, and I would like to take this opportunity to thank the Scottish Arts Council for their generosity in giving me a Writer's Bursary which helped to pay for the time needed to complete this book.

Some of the poems in this volume have already appeared in anthologies, as follows: "The Piano-tuner" in *New Poetry 2* (Arts Council of Great Britain, 1972); "Wood-nymph", in *Trees*, edited by Angus Ogilvie (The Stirling Gallery, December 1975); "Quality of Northernness", in *Scottish Poetry 8* (Scottish Arts Council, Carcanet, 1975); "Fellow Passenger", in *New Poems 1973–74*, a PEN Anthology (Hutchinson, 1974); "Trick of Memory", in *Poetry Dimension Annual 4*, edited by Dannie Abse (Robson Books, 1976), and "The Kite Kings", "Mountain Blaw", "The Ermine" and "The Salmon-Leap", all in *Poetry Introduction 3* (Faber & Faber, 1975). Other poems in this volume have appeared in *The Scotsman*, *Outposts* magazine and *Scottish International*, or have been broadcast by the BBC.

Ruby Tiger Land

They live in ruby tiger land.
Hers the stroke that slays,
hers the sun that draws
and devours live eyesight.

Moth-dusk evenings
swag the peacocks in royal blue
from tree to tree in India,
cry their evening cry:

"Miaou – aou – aou",
companion to the tiger.
He gives his ruby roar
in the sallow grasses below.

He flames steady flame
– not blackash as the boar
who bristles among roots,
shows his scoriated tushes.

The sambhur buck starts and bugles.
Feel a presentiment of game,
a knowledge that they are close by
before you see them.

Why do you do them this way,
land? – you hill goddess
with rubied eyepits, and coated in
the many colours of rosewood forest.

Dearly

I can love anything.
Among the runts of a ruined abbey
I spied, high up,
one of the vault bosses
belonging to the twelfth century:

head of a man
with bloodsuckers
at the eyes and mouth.

In that broad visage
they clamped at the edge of the eyes,
they clung to the corners of the mouth.
Here was a trove
for my heart's museum.

I wanted to offer him
a match to singe off
those leeches.

On the contrary,
he was in there first,
his hollowed stone eyesockets
gazing to burn
bloodgold lips in my face.

Sangam, Mysore State

i

Sunset fabrics centuries
in Sangam, that is a place
I wrapped time in a hug.
Footbeats derelict the river steps
into clovesmelling stone
hollowed by hard breasts of water.
Twinned swollen rivers,
both branches of the Cauvery,
run high and up against each other,
link arms in a reel of whirlpools.
They course for fleeing rocks,
rain bowstrung splinters of light
on their retreating stone flanks.
Cauvery's goddesses are tall enough
to beach crocodiles on the skyshore.

ii

Petals crack the plaster
of the steps' shrine.
Two beggars drag
leperlimbs along dust,
shake aluminium palms at me.
I have a hand for each tin,
my flesh coins the sore metal,
arms flow back to the loneness of my body.
I have no bruises,
I am Cauvery,
branchbodied,
singlestreamed,

because beggars' lifted hands
put blessing and rich silt
to bathe through my veins.

The Kite Kings

Each window spasms out
to a stretch of rooftops,
perches peopled by children.
To every boy, a kite,
crossed twigs and blue paper
lashed close by thread.
Each hour a kite,
each kite a tug
that links the boy
by twine to the sky's pull.

Only when he runs hard
will the kite float
without fall or droop
till it rivals the fleet
yellowhead vulture alongside.
Roofcaught tatter of lavender,
stick-and-
   string-and-
      paper bodied
boy, you are far and away
the frailest of kite kings.

A onearmed child teases
at the end of a string
a sunset coloured like
the juice of mango.
High out of the sun's rags
just a crossbar survives
to keep the shape of a bird,
some crucifix that courses
to the current of all winds.
What weal
the thrust of its thread
makes through the kite king's palm!

Patriot

Nadir, Nadir Shah
leaves the forest
where he lay
concealed.

And is he new?

In change of mind's possession,
blueribbed his breastcage,
feathered his heart's
whud and banged flapping.

And is he winged?

Flack, flacking across plaited treetips
he comes out to deliver his country,
flying turquoise as a shoal of parrots
airborne by their own fierce jibes.

The Gun

Your handsomeness will not relinquish
its poem; it never puts a finish

to the captive words, but hobbles them
until their feel for freedom deadens.

Sight and balance coordinate the whole
of you, you aim with nerved control.

You keep both eyes open and follow through
the arc of the poem's flight, to bring it low.

Marked, maimed, but not yet killed,
the poem shakes a fettered will,

admires your hammerless uncluttered line,
the gunmetal hardness of your mind,

and with an appropriateness of silver
makes overture of peace's quiver.

It attempts to chase the straight stock
of your smooth beauty, to silver its shot

and to damascene the surface
of your bright body. But

Your handsomeness will not relinquish
its poem; while it fires, it vanquishes.

Stars are Suns

By day, they are hidden in the lit air,
air which scatters light over the whole sky.

Soon after sunset one shines in the west.
Soon before sunrise shines another in the eastern sky.

One may be a sun star, one a dark planet;
they approach from both directions.

Here we might take observations of them,
But what navigator chooses bearings by their latitude?

My worldly heart alone finds them akin to it,
and asks them now to turn away men's wrath.

Most of all, to the planet I address myself,
she differs from the true star, and is my patron:

she gives off no light of her own, shines only
because she reflects his light falling on her.

When these bodies, whitehot and heavenly,
fall through the air to earth,

Their reputation begins to make
men turn and look back as they pass.

Inland stood high woods and forests,
but by Kincardine mudflats
we passed the ships' graveyard,
a shallow grove all of stumps.

Boats' ribs lie to and line the shore,
their sinew beached, ground for a spine,
and fleshed in stagnant brown:
"– just such a company of bones

as those," I said, "oh see
how I will be
one day through
waiting long for you."

You'd had plain seafaring
and your rashness
made bold to answer me,
"I have you as you are;

and what we do
is done in despite of
bones that have been bleached,
those longwintering skeletons."

The heart is a coracle
and slews around, its worn hide
tautened on a frame without keel,
it cannot obey the helm.

Yet I'll seajourney, I swear
to love you by season,
to live the skeleton's life,
to weather-expose this hunger.

Identifying You

What on earth
compares with you?

Not the sun who
is close to the eastern
edge of things.
Your eyes regard him, unblinking.

Not the moon who
comes with dark and
does great damage.
You make shards of her vessel.

Not the wind who
roars like a blast
from the blessed land.
You keep this place warm against him.

Not the rain who
whispers our sins are
refusals to get wet.
Your hair gives colour to dry-stacked hay.

Not our children who
are frosthaloed stars
brightening us by delusions.
You have a wintry way with you.

What on the earth
compares with you?

Clouds and Clay

Between the cloud and the ground
a harmony is seen, as turbulence
shapes the hills again in air.

These gunmetal greys and whites
indicate the swollen earth below,
where basic rock soars in an upcurrent.

The hill is a wellbent shoulder
to toll the clouds like bells:
hemispheres peal in set carillon.

The hills, the clouds make chords
– until a wind veer scatters them,
sets notes ajar, breathes on the looking-glass.

The country's image in the atmosphere
flies in pieces. At last, only one man's bearing
is left to give away the shape of the land's spirit.

For Scotland is spur hills and long hollows
and in that hollow mould she cast him
to be her clay in ideal conformation.

Outwith City Limits

It is dead things, and the nearly dead
that interest vultures most.

As griffon vultures surround and overlap
closewinged, their precious carcase,

With a deep reach the memory can penetrate
to hack its bill inside the corpse;

Thoughts wrench my flesh to manageable pieces
and, drunk on putrefaction, hop away.

Who would have thought an old love
might ever be the skeleton at the feast?

The Greyhound

Often I use the quickturning quarry's art
To reach the reclusion of my heart.

Yet He comes on like a longbacked hound
Able to stand over a lot of ground,

Free running like the scytheswing of a mower
His action shows great driving power.

His is the sound formation I would liken
To whatever God has made breathtaking.

A muscular and balanced grace
Can cleanly run, back doubling to the pace,

That back like a beam, head of a snake
– So the good greyhound shows his make.

A heart has room in that chest, nerved
In deep underline to form a curve.

Shoulderblades laid back over the lungs' panting
Set sharp bones in angulation long and slanting,

Articulate to bring the length of leg in line.
Concussion of the earth speeds him up an incline.

The thoroughbred throws forward low and straight
Those forelegs with unstilted gait.

That supple neck can reach to level-bite
The swerving flanks of prey in flight.

Out from among a world of beauties, God sent
The longdog to grip my mind with what He meant.

Magdalene Wonders

How well you know
– not just to resuscitate
my four day dead brother –
when I want you.

Tears make you simple,
yourself come out into the open
like a handsome boy
scuffing bare feet along the roadside.

Then the translucency of skin
with tears coursing above it!
White fantail doves tilt
in flock to the first leaves.

Untwining a blanch thin cotton
off my brother's face (its brass discolour)
a slow compassion of your hand drew
across as dawn pinks the sands.

You beat down my eyes by beauty.
Your smile finds its way to my throat.
I can no more love in a timelag
than *you* could hold out to mourn.

John

Paraphrase 1

John wanders, in loose clothes,
intent to draw God's touch,
and sings of how it is to be
a psalmist of the natural.

Heretics are like this.

Water has no place here
except as baptism,
he handles each head below it
as an aster caught in hoarfrost.

Each drop is forced
into a boretide by the good man John.
Who cares to keep his head
above that watercourse?

The rigour of his walking
through a desert
made it seem
parkland of amaranth.

Harbinger John
found wilderness
proportionate to
his great heart.

Heretics are like this.

Deerhounds

Admit the lives more valuable
than our life, than the bodies we bear
more beautiful: tall grey dogs,

what huntsman, what dogboy loosed you
on our slow hearts
and let you slaughter them?

Long dogs, you move with air
belling the vault of your ribcage.
You subdue the miles below your hocks.

Levelled out in speed across wayless country,
over the open grassmoor that is paradise,
the onset of your going undulates the ground.

The bracken hurdles below your height,
the rushes make way for you;
your hard eyes hold in sight the rapid hills.

Brace of deerhounds, a matched two!
Intent, all flame, is what quickens
those long throats thonged with leather.

The Salmon-Leap

Salmon, clean-run from new seas,
Blue-black and black-spotted, locking in an eddy
Prior to making his curve of a fish-leap:
Now rose-gill rising, ready
To hoop a steady
Bend above floodgate.
With his short taper tail's rapid hiss
The sock-eye enters. Water closes on fish.

Lover, newly arrived in fresh sight
As silverskin of atlantic littoral, descend midair
To keep my eyes under strike; plunging through,
Here salmon-leap, there
Dive, there
My regard is water smooring over the mark of you.
Implant upon my gaze headlong your lineaments;
Like sphincter muscle, depths close around them and
clench.

The Design

Watch how love's oppression
forces me to wording you.
The poem has a surrender in it.

I have tried to use it
to sketch a map of the countries
that I envision in your bed.

I could not trace on its skin
the rock veined with rose quartz
set in deep as your sinews.

Through the flat of my hand
I acquaint myself with that smoothness,
its wellknit surfaces like yours.

On here I'll try each word
with a bold vigilance
– so the Pict drew on stoneface

the line of wolf's breastbone
outjutting,
the line of wolf's loin, loping.

He put down that free flow
by chiselling, and so I know there
must be some wording to fit you.

The Fiery Hill

It was mirk-dark
by the time the hill came up.
That one night
there were brush fires through its forest.

The throng of pinetrees
were like grey conglomerate rock
split open to discover garnets,
to set off its reds.

17

This same night,
kindling the combustible dark,
I lie by night with you,
uncovering hidden nests of fire.

I think before dawn
bright skin can but corrode to blisters
and molten membrane come to ash,
a conflagration of marrow.

We do not flinch,
nor does such fire
make us shrink from it.
We are homed on the fiery hill.

For the Poet Lanny Miller

You, Lanny, you
have done what I could not do;
never got a return ticket
for any place you have gone to.

Like the hill fires in March
you are the true visionary,
reaching to the tangent of extremes,
burning out the atrophied roots,
and after you have been that way
set free the aromatic scorch of peat.

18

Eyes turn to the look of light in you
– that's what it means
just to be one moment's beauty in the blood
and to make it last for
the raggedy phoenix
of loving-kindness
which would not be afraid
to perch on your wrist
and shake its feathers free of ash.

The Love God

Once there was no love;
then, when love did appear,
he was rather different from the other gods.

He didn't come out of a shell
or float up from the sea.
As he walked on the canal path

he was there at my side:
a black godling rose
out of an open sewer.

A young madrasi, he was coated
with tar to protect his flesh
from the slime's contagion.

Where you'd have thought
only the dead could have floated,
he came up with one supple move.

He was of this world,
one of the very low
yet one of the divinely beautiful.

For if the badlooking are bad
and the goodlooking are good,
then that makes him a god,

a black steatite statue:
my copy
for more than one love.

Quality of Northernness

India's every dawn
never differs,
flashes out by appointment:
except, seasons are wet
or not,
or have plenty of south in their gale.

The same dance
and the same chant
is danced or chanted
to the rising sun
by the millenium.
If you want a different dawn you'll be lucky.

Just once
my morning had it all,
the all of every cardinal
compass-point there is.
Cold white mists wandered
you and I up against the back of the palace.

By mistake
her white residence
reared up at us:
a newly dead queenmother herself,
this Yuvrani wrapped in stiff shawls
was signal of our extreme southernness.

She had the flap of abandoned sails.
An interior deserted:
ruinous dancing-hall,
staircase treacherously fine,
lengthy mirrors telling stained truths,
cabinets emptied of English porcelains.

Only white pillars on the outside
lasted to be solid; daybreak was no
longer the warm sacred swan of self-possession
floating south and south on a lotus dawn;
it was, instead, a white icy ship
whaling through an arctic sea.

The prow of somewhere cooler
hove to at dawn
to break and sink us like icefloes:
whatever northernness was in that graveyard,
it buried us north and south
as a believer does a dead blanched heretic.

A Night Remorse

At nightfall we walk out with courser
dogs to pursue the hare.
Running together, they will be wind driving water

we hope, as from the black green of the wood
our pair stalk out, their horned masks
with tassels seeming like hawks in hood.

For these deep-bodied dogs are right
hounds who will fix on a hare
and follow him by sight,

and him only, past all others, then
through whole grazing herds
still know and kill *him*.

Here the buck hare comes, making
his traverse of the highroad,
dawdling through the mottled evening.

He clears the hedge-gap,
seeking his form in soft matgrass,
longing to hunch up in earth's lap.

We eagerly hurry to hunt him,
with dogs on slip-leash
and bending out of view beyond the road-brim,

while he pauses to breathe, stiff,
– when the car comes between us:
he wheels round, mistaken, turns as he's hit.

Death by metal and vulcan-rubber.
He is uptorn by wheelrims
who might have been rooted as a lover

in our fixed thought, coursed and known
and singled out. That's different from this destruction
which grips us with a night remorse worse than talon.

Fellow Passenger

Mister B. Rajan, diamond buyer,
crystallises from this travelling companion.
He goes by rail, it seems, by criss
and cross, Hyderabad to Bangalore
to Madras, Madras, Madras,
seeking the industrial diamond.

He brings new orient gems from hiding.
Himself, he wears goldwealthy rings
of ruby, and, for fortune,
another of God Venkateswaran.
His smile is a drillpoint diamond's,
incisive his kindness.

Sparrowboned, he walks unstable passageways,
living on boiled eggs and lady's-fingers
with noggins of whisky to follow.
He dreams of his house, the shrineroom picture
of Sai Baba, corkscrew-haired young saint.
And he has at home beautiful hidden daughters.

Sheet lightning of an evening
lights the jungle from rich dark.

The first damp of the year
claps to wake a thousand flying-foxes.

Thunder groans and butts its horns,
the impassioned start of bucks.

Clouds downpour upon an hourgreen dust,
the moment's gallop and the musk of deerherds.

These creatures thrive by rainfall,
they hustle and press through the forest.

Sheared off by thunderbolt
their progeny shall be sturdy,

For so they ask their native prince,
the albino elephant, the lord in light rosespots.

An elephant is a rain cloud
who walks on earth.

He is cloud-fabricating,
a monument in grey, binding monsoonclouds.

He conjures his fellow-monsoon
to approach, by whiteness irresistible.

The albino tosses and turns the hills,
for without him the grassblade sleeps.

The hill has a life of its own.
Fish! fish! it whales its way
through the sky,
dashing clouds off
with the temper
of a granite fin.

The hill owns its life.
Dog! dog! it ripples a collar
of pine-studs,
bristles its hipbones
through bracken;
mist froths its jowls.

The Splice

The cob swan died homing at velocity
on telegraph wire-lines. With rapidity
his death tautened strands of the heart,
tying him with a splice white knot.
His bill split to the throat, back
splintering the length of yellow beak.

That loose flap must weather away eventually,
leaving a swan's breastbone by the sea.
The sternum that was his ship-keel
become lozenge-shaped like an ancient shield
pocked with holes, its spinnaker breath
will prove sail-hollow, light as a broad leaf.

Still, where he winged her memory, she hesitates
on resplendent water beside her dead mate;
a pure white light – one of a former pair.
For three days, among a raft of floating seabirds there
she weaves a threadline offshore from deathless
feathers, keeps watch on a sky emptied and cheerless.

The Ermine

Cub, you curl in your first sleep
since birth, creaking as a hinge would too
if it were link and bracket
of the two worlds, like you.

A mother so vigilant,
bolt nightlong upright
and wakeful atop a snowbank of starch
I grow pale as winter camouflage fur comes white.

So stoatlike, I hold my head up,
always presenting the face
to you, polecat's young,
where you lie landwide as innocence.

Embroidered on the lining
of my left sleeve, at a glance
I seem to wear the eyes and ears
of ermine, signifying vigilance.

"Passing"

Child, when I get
a glimpse of your skin, so far
coloured like tawny sarcenet,
I think of how you will pass in Asia

for some fair brahmin boy
with features fine-drawn
to set off eyes charred as the berry
glowing among sloe-thorns.

For that, you'll be welcome in India,
"passing" as Kim did once
through inner temples or among shahs:
Europeans looking through you like a halfcaste.

For you, the bay waves can come in musical
and big, the old shore
and the old stars look recognisable
to you: for three centuries or more

you have sat the logs of that katamaran,
one of those which rode out to the sailingships
when the British could not come in closer than
the lines of breakers. You smile with Śiva's lips

to see the moon rise and spin her *charka*.
Who cares if the wheel be independence that she spins?
The subcontinent threads silk yarn around you
as tightly as if you were her bobbin.

River Talk

"Give us the Himavathy river for drinking,
Cauvery river for bathing in," they say,
the local people. They drank yesterday,
so today go downstream on the Cauvery,

slow, certain as currents, they surely know
the day flows when Ganga is here,
the mother goddess, to visit Cauvery the fair
as she does each Indian river in turn through the year.

Cauvery herself is a silt-heavy goddess
who clashes in blue with brown; reeds
on her banks, mango-topes above floods.
She goes skinny-dipping, no hour so sportful and free,

river cradling and swinging the swimmer's body.
After, long-poling upstream in the dugout, the lean
fishers punt back to the riversteps. They have seen
more than kite catch carp, or white spiderlilies tendril
                                                    streams.

The Piano-tuner

Two hundred miles, he had come
        to tune one piano, the last hereabouts.
Both of them were relics of imperial time:
        the Anglo-Indian and the old upright knockabout.

He peered, and peered again
    into its monsoon-warped bowels.
From the flats of dead sound he'd beckon
    a tune on the bones out to damp vowels.

His own sounds were pidgin.
    The shapeliness of his forearms
lent his body an English configuration,
    but still, sallow as any snakecharmer

he was altogether piebald.
    Far down the bridge of his nose
perched roundrimmed tortoiseshell spectacles;
    his hair, a salt-and-pepper, white foreclosed.

But he rings in the ear yet,
    his interminable tapping of jarring notes:
and, before he left,
    he gave point to those hours of discord.

With a smile heavenly
    because so out of place, cut off from any home there,
he sat down quietly
    to play soft music: that tune of "Beautiful Dreamer",

a melody seized from yellowed ivories
    and rotting wood. A damper
muffled the pedal point of lost birthright. We eaves-
    dropped on an extinct creature.

Hibernator

My child's flesh, after the bath,
smells sweet as the thaw
must, to hibernating creatures.

While I washed him
I was the winter-wind in action
of attrition: he emerged a landform.

Now, drying him with the bleached towel,
I am that she-bear who licks her cub,
moulding it to its true shape to come.

For a Son's First Birthday

You were a Moses striking rock.
I let out the life
that wanted to come.

What I forget
is that restiveness:
there was the true childbed.

I watched the back of your head come:
that much form
let me know you were a son.

No bald pate, but a full head of hair;
the appearance of your scalp unfolding
the reality of a new mind within.

Born wringing wet as the moorlands,
you were blue
as blaeberry behind their leaves.

Your first breath
blew you up so pink
you were ragged robin in the marshes.

What I forget
is your first sound:
loud, brilliant and reedy.

The Negative

He's come for the pipe-band,
being just big enough
to put on his sporran.
My son is a scrap
of his own tartan:
he is all kilt, save for his brown knees
and the bloodied old scars on them.

It's his everyday kilt, but here, today,
it makes a tourist trample through the crowd:

"Move *there*, little boy."
She fires the camera, conspires
to steal his virtue into a picture.
He flashes a dour and warring glance
that must be perfect for her.

31

Now that it's taken, he ought
to spring to life,
flash out a knife,
ask for her money or the negative.
Yet he must know
that will develop into something
different from the youthful Lachlan.

No,
the negative will show
a stony moor,
a twisted tree,
and all around them
the ragged map
of Scotland.

Sold a Pup

From off dog-benches loud with fights
and bulking large as Golan Heights
trotted the silver person of a whippet
moulded like laboratory-glass pipettes.

A shade too highly bred,
and single in its purpose as a copperhead,
it was showing its paces for any buyer
who might want beauty to go by in a blur.

My wishful thinking now recalled
here was what I always wanted most of all.
See, it was spoke-legged with splinter bone
and ribbed with spotted flank like a fawn!

I bid and outbid all competitors
to buy it from some tonsured dealer
shifty as thieving moon. I took the warm
leather of its leash, thin and live as mealworm,

To draw it homewards, with treble
knots in the line to make it biddable:
but its hard and skinny joints began to melt
as warm air dissolved the metallic pelt

I had just purchased dearly.
Those thirty pounds taxed me severely
for, reading lot number and name when it was sold
I saw "My Sick Soul" was what the bitch was called.

Casting a Shoe

The child I could see
was one of mine, yesterday,
by the way he had some aptitude
for being in place, at the appointed
spot of earth to celebrate
and join in the random miracle.

Small as he was, his scalp crawled
to hear a first fore-sound of it,
the fast approach of a cantering milk-float
loaded up with top-heavy mortality.
It crated a hundred bottles sucked dry
and left rinsed milky as sea-glass.

He shivered, hearing the strange knock,
the unique clang in amongst many hoofbeats
that signals a loose shoe.
Going home fast, scared stablewards,
the halfwit milkman
whipped up discords.

Sent like a coin scudded along ice
the shining crescent of the shoe
skimmed to my child's feet,
gave him the nailhead's hard wink,
and put a halt to the tender
unshod hoof in the roadway.

From his on-high of milky cloud
the charioteer, daft boy, dismounted
heavily: in the blue bag of his overalls
he swaggered like a stray bullock
in sodden bogland, shying wall-eyed
from jumping over even this castoff moon.

Yet, at a shambles of a run,
his crumpled head to one side,
he snatched up the iron new-moon
of the sloughed shoe; at the same time
he lit all the waxwhite blanks of his face
at the sun's run-rosin fire of the child's stare.

The Crook-maker

One day it would come into my grandfather's mind
to make a crook and staff.
A shepherd friend had sent
rams' horns for him to give the proper shape.

First, he looked through Scotland's woods
for the single stock in a spread of trees
as far as Blair Atholl, rejecting stick after stick,
looking for the straightest hazel bough.

Then there were days, maybe three,
of turning the incurved twists of the horn
into the single crooked claw of their hooked form:
to one smooth bend like a unique curl of hair.

It unbent through steeping in hot water.
He used his vice-grip to hold it to the curve.
He carved and whittled it to an adorned head,
a curving salmon-leap or a fluffed thistle-top.

He bound crook and staff with loops
of a thick turk's-head knot,
a red turban of twine. All this time
he had never noticed his other walks or work.

But the longest time of all was to come,
smoothing and polishing the crook,
adding each day to its sheen, from
the first emery paper to the last chamois leather.

It changed from angry ruts to fondled silks.
He put on the ferrule last,
tipped the wood with a metal tip,
signing it as of a man's making.

With the finishing stroke put to the work
there sprang up before our eyes
a bough with new proportions,
sprouting a curly horn, blossoming a carving.

The heap of shavings
was still fresh at his feet:
my grandfather not a moment older
through all these days of crook-making.

Woodnymph

The dryad is composing in the dark.
She lies upright, in the vertical
of a tree among the grove of oak.
She chooses to inhabit all
the wildwood and the wilderness;
once inside a treetrunk she will
cajole her motor nerves to stillness.

Now her tendons draw up a fibrous frame,
her ligaments bind a twisted grain,
she can metamorphose her blood
to a pink streak in dark green wood.
Her thighs' concentric circles stand
extending to the bark their annual band

of light and dark; each light one springwood,
the dark is summer growth. She should
find her collarbone acts as a strut
to keep the shoulder-branches out,
while her hands, carved in relief
as a natural oakleaf
twig verses out of the sky.
She sees less with the open eye.

And that is why
she is blindly composing,
knowing the poems to be coming,
darting through the air;
they are swifts; here and there,
making the movement characteristic
of the bird in flight, they flick
past with open mouths, feeding by wing-flex
on flies and insects.
They follow the tree, as she doubles
back into the dark: good poets remain supple.

Eyewitnesses

No-one takes their eyes from three-month me.
My every smile is their heliograph
– a message sent from the mountain.

Two glassblowers make me these burning-glasses:
a green glazier and one of brown
stain the lenses, blur to a bombshell grey.

For the day that decides my eyes' colouring
is put off again:
who can have their shade named?

They are seas in continual aesture and vexation,
the then and there of green,
the here and now of brown.

Colours hold uneasy truce in them,
I make a sheet of Scottish water
sink in the deluge of my stare.

Round hill, far sea –
all eyes are led to my features.
My beauty alters and shines like a drake's neck.

Mountain Blaw

When I came into my own
it was at some five years old
going to the Mountain Blaw farm
in a barren cold.

Its roofs were long as a javelin,
a projectile poised by the winter wind,
lying on the ruck of ridge for muscle,
that shoulder ruche-pleated by streams in ice-hustle.

The house smoked up strange fantail doves
composed of snow; to a fledgeling poet
it read as a first draft attempt at love,
steaming out its opacity kettle-hot.

Old bee-skeps, and the cows in byre
Spelled milk and honey would be there.
The steading looped like briar in a figure-eight
to twine me with my whereabouts that night.

With storm-lamp and pail of hot bran mash
I went into dark black as horse-treacle
to feed the new grey racing mare, our first.
But outside the loosebox, something quicksilver fickle

– the farm itself – rose sudden as mercury
through a vein, a sense of place saturating
me. Face radiant, the halter held upward of my hand,
I ran home, a spy returned from that Promised Land.

Rising Early

Rising early, I can remember
what it was like
when I had a child's eye level,
only so high above the ground.

In that dimension
I felt the walled garden
as no adult can do,
for I had to tilt my head
right back, to see
my grandmother's window.

The many other windows
in the building seemed
stunned by their smoke of emptiness,
but in hers, a dull yellow
shone around her.
Her hand so active
at the sink, paused, and waved.

Right up to today
I am the same girl
to my grandmother.
The love between us travels across
in a moving whole of silence
like any bird,
and as if surrounded
by the high window-way glow,
we are only a wave apart.

For Maeve

In music that's the pure karnatic,
a song takes two hours to sing.
Like a birth, there's no time to it,
no past, no future,
not even a present.

I heard twin brothers sing,
black Tamil throats in unison
trilling through every quarter-tone:
it took them ten minutes
to sing the name of god.

They frayed the word out
to show each thread in its silk.
Half an hour for a sentence.
I welcomed its close
like the final pang of birth.

"Vishnu slept . . .
on his ocean of milk . . .
dreaming . . .
his creation of the world."
I believed in timelessness by then.

Years after, I remembered them;
at a birth fresh from that same ocean,
my daughter was washed ashore
with curds still covering her head,
creamy-white from the warm amniotic sea.

So swift her birth, she brought with her
upon her body the eternal buttermilk
that had coated it in the womb:
a small Venus rising, she hummed, then,
a dozen grace notes to fill out her name:
        "Maeve, the intoxicating."

The Small Flame

I never flamed at a set time
upwards from child to woman;
no, I hung fire for years, to find
out how death works.
At tomboy twelve, poaching lurked
in me, in my hard hands,
thick cap of hair, those heavy boots.

My tattered jacket was stolen
off someone else's scarecrow in the field;
its pockets were a thicket, hemmed
in wire snares, of cartridges and knife,
I'd carry home a hare larger than life
across the moor, and not yield
to the pain of holding him up at shoulderheight.

Between the coatflap and my ribs there lay
a four-ten, the folding shotgun:
it took life at so few yards, that one,
I had to stalk up the whiskers of my prey.
When I spent the summer lying there
in the cornfield with the boy a year
older than me, it was to snipe at birds.

But the day a rabbit leapt into my hand,
twisting away from the collie's teeth,
and I carried it live underneath
my arm, to set it free on the moorland,
I felt my body white as a flame's inside;
as if, myself snared, hot wire swung me high.
I didn't go to meet the boy at dusk.

For Surah

I always had a dog,
but you were the one
who embodied my own spirit.
I would love to have been you;
simple, swift, beautiful
till the day you died.

I picture myself as you:
cherished and important
throughout five thousand years
since the first cave-painter at Balk
held back the deerhound tightly.

I want to see you again
as you were, looking straight at me.
Perhaps a red pollen of blood.
dusts your muzzle, in heaven;
perhaps some hare in eternity
scents a hound on the little breeze.

If it should run from you
as you are, the hare's heart will burst,
immortal or not; you are off the leash
now, who kept death on a tether
tied to you; where you went,
death and beauty ran together.

Shopping

Shopping women used to get in my way,
with that habit they have
of suddenly stopping,
or rushing to one side.
Now I am one of them:
my feet trail over the pavements
like theirs,
and I'm hungry for new price-tags.

Almost, I am one of them.
Don't believe
I am altogether what I look,
for I feel
these doorposts and striped awnings
are the slender tousled trees
of a hilly jungle.
Paper money and coins fall into my palm
with the rustle and drop of a tree-viper.

Most of all, it's when
I am bearing home a fat string bag
with the sure haul and pace
of a panther dragging her deer
that I know
another shopper's stray child
will keep up alongside
my own cubs,
to run with me
like a hopeful wild-dog.

Trick of Memory

Three years north
of the tropic of cancer
have changed me.
I no longer put oil on my head
or sew jasmine, to sleep with it in my hair.
I pinch shut the letters from India:
their language seems wrinkled
as the features of cholera.
It is difficult to picture their writer,
crosslegged on a teak swing indoors.

I used to long for a pair
of the silver toe-rings worn by women
married into the princely family.
Now their faint sound would seem
unattainable as a skein of geese.
I used to love the royal blue
of the two-tone sun-and-shade
silk sari worn by the mothers
of pretty boys named Dilip or Ajoy.
Now that blue would seem
remote as a piece of sky.
I do not care to remember
what husband might entitle me to toe-rings,
or what son would have sent me peacock saris.

45